To Charles Barnes Jr. and Myral & Loa Clark–
who first turned our hearts.

—Charlotte and Jonah

Text © 2022 Charlotte and Jonah Barnes
Illustrations © 2022 Olena Tkachenko
All rights reserved.

No part of this book may be reproduced in any form whatsoever, whether by graphic, visual, electronic, film, microfilm, tape recording, or any other means without prior written permission of the publisher, except in the case of brief passages embodied in critical reviews and articles.

This is not an official publication of The Church of Jesus Christ of Latter-day Saints. The opinions and views expressed herein belong solely to the author and do not necessarily represent the opinions or views of Cedar Fort, Inc. Permission for the use of sources, graphics, and photos is also solely the responsibility of the author.

ISBN 13: 978-1-4621-4317-7

Published by CFI, an imprint of Cedar Fort, Inc.
2373 W. 700 S., Springville, UT 84663
Distributed by Cedar Fort, Inc., www.cedarfort.com

Library of Congress Control Number for softback edition: 2021949111

Cover design and typesetting by Shawnda T. Craig
Cover design © 2022 Cedar Fort, Inc.

Printed in the United States of America

10 9 8 7 6 5 4 3 2 1

Printed on acid-free paper

To the grown-up readers:

This book is about the wee person beside you,
so show them and tell them,
"There's history inside you!"

If they learn your history and make it their own,
then those little people will never feel alone.
Because families grow and strengthening starts
by sharing your stories and turning little hearts.

You can do it.

—Charlotte and Jonah Barnes

Looks

If you look around at people today,
they all look so different, wouldn't you say?
There's some with big ears
and some with green eyes.
There's big and there's small
and there's every size.

Speaking of which, where'd you come by that nose?
No one has ears or a nose quite like those.

No one on Earth!
Does that make you feel good?
Good to be special?
Unique? Well, it should!

But where did you get them?
Who gave you your looks?
You can't find the answer
in movies or books.
You'll have to look back
and up and inside.
Through years, up a tree,
to an earlier time.
Your ancestors gave you
your hips and your toes.
And somebody back there
bequeathed you that nose!

It's time you begun, it's time that you wondered
whose teeth or long toes or square jawline you plundered.
You can't pay them back for the good looks you took.
Just thank them by viewing an old photo book.
Peruse a few pictures. Can you pick out you?
Your forelookers' looks are inside you, it's true!
Of all the Earth's people, you are totally rare.
And it's thanks to your ancestors hiding back there.

Immigration

Begin from the start.
Where was your starting?
It's likely your starting
began with a parting.

Your foregoers probably
left an old home.
Did you think they just
sprang from the grass
like a gnome?

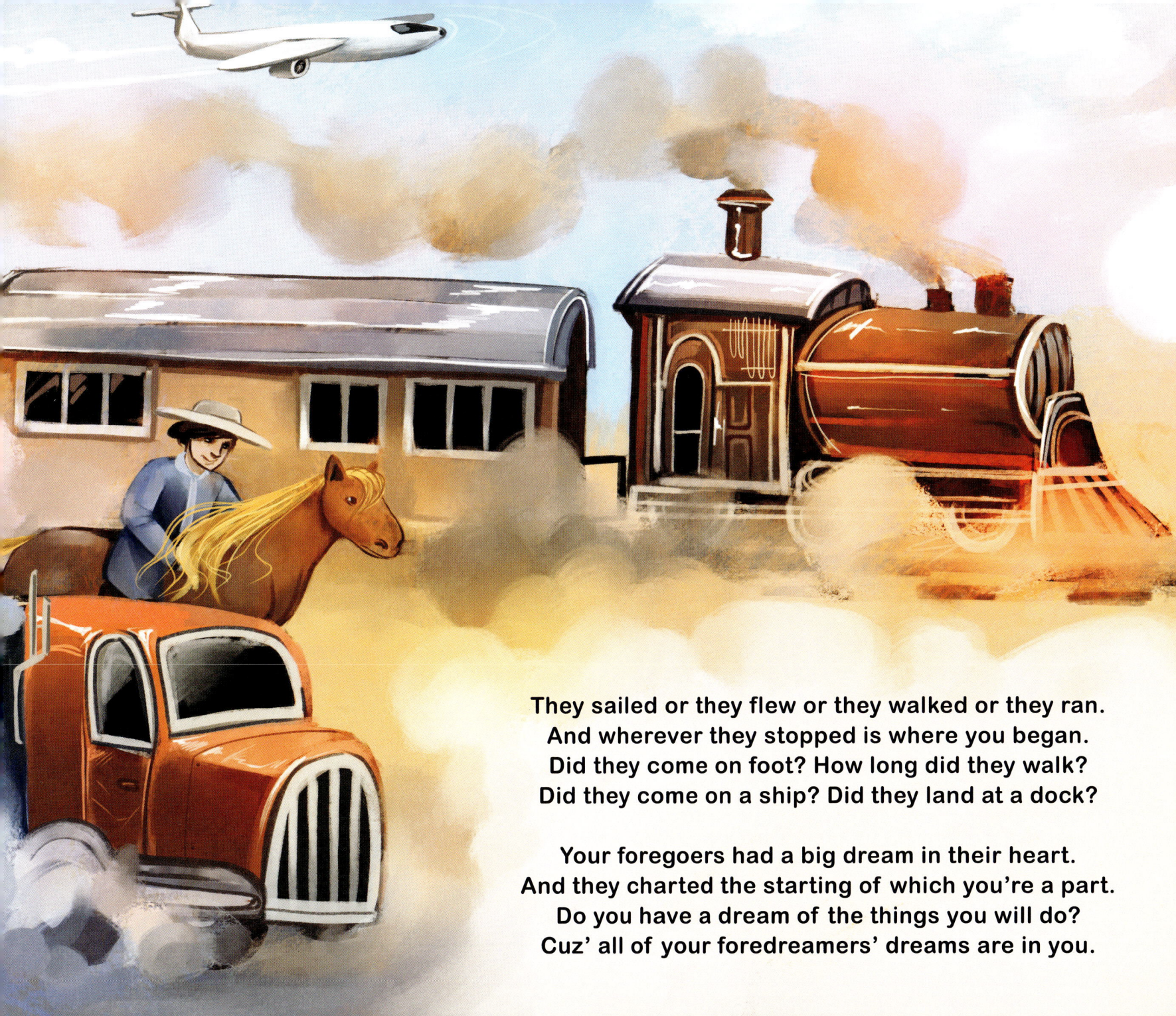

They sailed or they flew or they walked or they ran.
And wherever they stopped is where you began.
Did they come on foot? How long did they walk?
Did they come on a ship? Did they land at a dock?

Your foregoers had a big dream in their heart.
And they charted the starting of which you're a part.
Do you have a dream of the things you will do?
Cuz' all of your foredreamers' dreams are in you.

Education

Before they learned books like the one you are reading,
your forefarmers farmed up the food you are eating
by muddling through math and learning each letter
your forebetters made their life better and better.
And since they worked hard and hoed you a row,
you're buried in blessings from the seeds that they sowed!

Music

Did your forefolks have maestros or singers or song?
Did they tootle the fife or bang on the gong?
Did music make Uncle Bob grow out his hair?
How long did your Aunt Myrtle play the first chair?

Perhaps there is rhythm inside of your mind from gifts that your foregivers left you behind.

Culture

Your people had interesting culture and foods.
Bright clothing, rich customs,
fast dances, deep moods.
How did they embrace? What foods did they chew?
I bet there is something there you'd enjoy too.
Like hats that are tall or cheese that is blue.
Or a drink that stinks or a hard wooden shoe.

Or flowers in hair
or dresses that swirl.
Or bowing, or kissing,
or beards that curl.
But how can you know
unless you go try it?

Try something of theirs,
their dress or their diet.
Your foretasters tastes
were groovy and new.
The sparks of their culture
still flicker in you.

Language

Did your ancestors give you their tongue,
do you think?
What I mean is your words,
not the thing that is pink.

If you met your foreparents and tried to converse,
they might wonder if you had been dropped by the nurse!
Because English to them just might sound like a joke.
Can you speak any speech from the language they spoke?

If it's different, don't worry. They still passed on tone.
Your inflection, your tenor, your pitch are on loan.
Yes, they sounded like you and you sound like them too.
Your ancestors' voices have echoes in you.

Tough Times

Have you ever been sad?
Or wanted to cry?
Have you thought,
"No one's ever been so sad as I!"

Well, not to be mean,
but frankly, they have.
You've had foremas and pas
who've been exactly that sad.
Your great-grandpas cried,
or maybe their mothers.
They fought with their sisters
or wrestled their brothers.

Their friends let them down.
Their feelings got bent.
Sometimes they gave up.
They felt totally spent.

Mistakes

Now sometimes your great-grands might not have been grand. They may have done oopsies you don't understand.

Don't cover your eyes if their deeds weren't ideal. Without the full story they do not feel real. They started like you, just a lil human pup. Like you, they had troubles— at times they messed up.

If you mess up too,
a pup you'll still be.
You're part of this pack:
you're in good company.
Life's not a race. Get used to mishap.
But learn from your forechaps.
They left you a map.

Discipline

Is your ice box running?
Could you run and catch it?
Do you know all the labor
your fam did to match it?
Did they dig big ice cellars?
Did they mine out black coal?

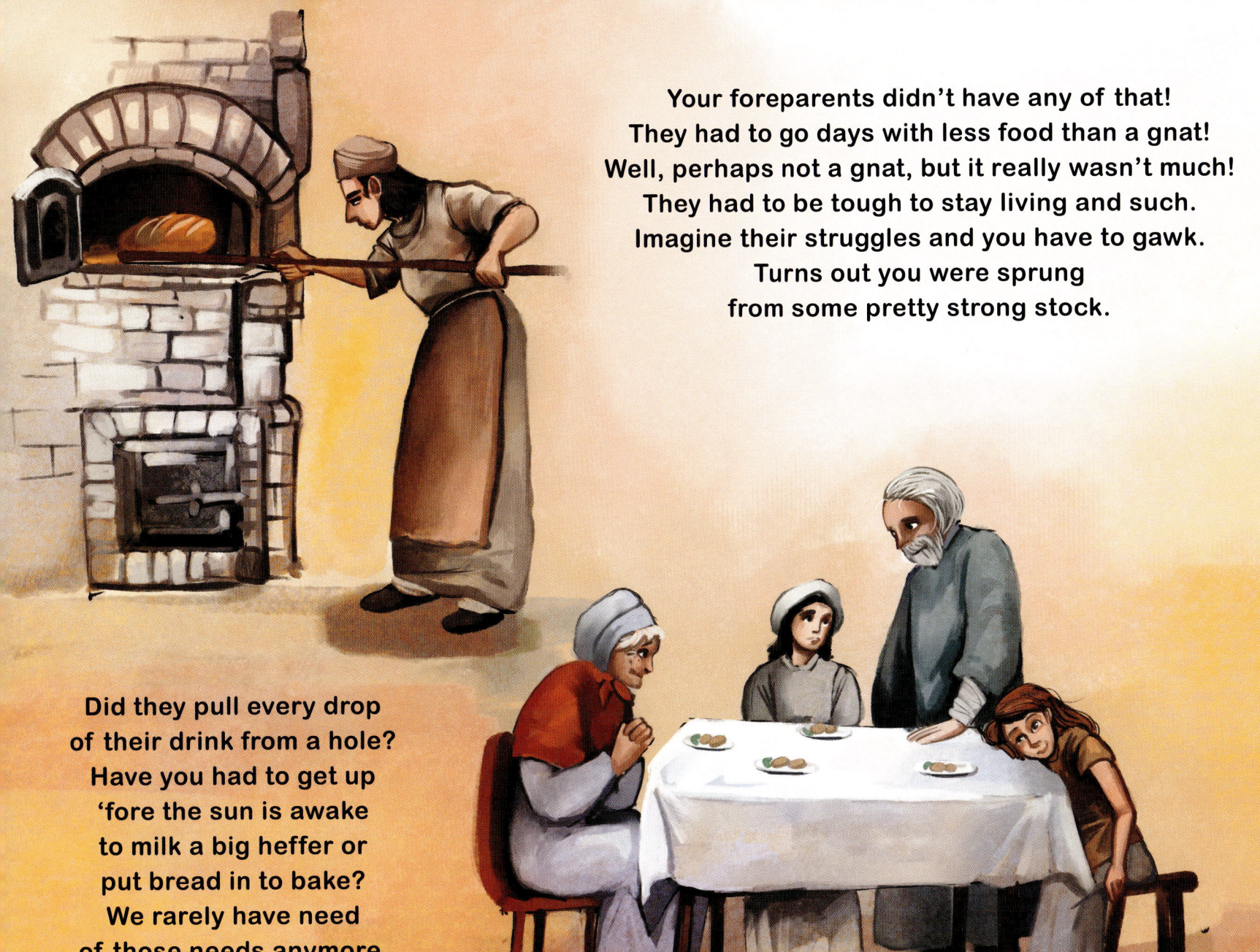

Your foreparents didn't have any of that!
They had to go days with less food than a gnat!
Well, perhaps not a gnat, but it really wasn't much!
They had to be tough to stay living and such.
Imagine their struggles and you have to gawk.
Turns out you were sprung
from some pretty strong stock.

Did they pull every drop
of their drink from a hole?
Have you had to get up
'fore the sun is awake
to milk a big heffer or
put bread in to bake?
We rarely have need
of those needs anymore.
We have ovens, and fridges,
and grocery stores.

Religion

My grandmother told me that faith can move nations.
Did faith ever move your religious relations?
Most people believe in a God up above
who teaches them honor, and mercy, and love.
And what they believed affected their deed,
the leader they'd heed, or the creed they would read.

They prayed on the mountains or down in a pew.
Do you have that faith? It's long overdue
to find out the churches that they belonged to
and whether it's one God, or three Gods, or two.
Your forefaithfuls fervently had faith in you.

Who You Are

From your ears to your toes, from your wits to your warts.
From music or dancing, to cooking or sports.
You're a verse in a song, a car on a train,
a floor on a house, a link in a chain.

People like you looked forward to you.
They thought of your life, and they wondered who
would wear their proud nose and carry their dream,
who'd step up and one day be head of their team.

That's you! You're uniquely made up of those guys!
Your life is a tapestry sewn of their lives.
See, you are your ancestors. You're special and rare.
So special that nobody else can compare.

So ask that tall person who read you this poem
for stories and tales and set out to know 'em!
Then you will see you from a new point of view,
'cuz you can't know you without knowing them too!

Discussion Questions

LOOKS: Which ancestors do you look like and how? What traits do you want to—or not want to—pass on to your children?

IMMIGRATION: What countries did your ancestors come from? How did they travel? What sequence of your ancestors' immigration got you to where you are today? Where do you think you and your future children may live one day?

EDUCATION: What stories do you know about your ancestors at school? Who was your first ancestor who went to college? What subjects did your ancestors study? How can your pursuit of a great education bless your future family?

MUSIC: Which of your ancestors were musical? Did they sing? What instruments did they play? Do you know a particular song an ancestor sang or played? What songs do you want to sing to your children?

CULTURE: What cultures did your ancestors enjoy? What aspects of their culture do you enjoy today (food, clothing, music, art, dances, traditions, holidays, etc.)? What parts of your culture are you excited to share with your future children?

LANGUAGE: What languages did your ancestors speak? Did they have a different accent? How hard do you think it was for them to learn a new language? Can you say anything in your ancestors' languages? What new words or phrases can you learn?

TOUGH TIMES: What were some disappointments, trials, heartaches, or struggles that your ancestors experienced? How did they overcome? How does knowing that your ancestors went through tough times help you as you go through tough times, too? When you're going through trials, how do you suppose your ancestors might advise you?

WAR: Which of your ancestors fought in wars? What were their experiences? Why do you suppose they fought? How can you honor their sacrifices? If no one in your family served in the military, then what experiences did your ancestors have just trying to live during a war?

MISTAKES: What are some mistakes that your ancestors made? Why did they make them? Have their mistakes affected you? Will your mistakes affect your children?

DISCIPLINE: What chores did your ancestors have as children or adults? How hard did they work at their various jobs? What are some hard things you have to do? How can your hard work bless your future children?

RELIGION: Do you know what religions your ancestors had? What did they believe and how did that affect their lives? How did their faith alter their choices? What religion are you? How will your religious beliefs and actions affect your future family?

Activity Ideas

LOOKS: Look at pictures of your ancestors and see what traits you share. Draw a picture of yourself and label those shared traits. Dress up and pose for a picture like that ancestor.

IMMIGRATION: Draw various ancestors' immigration routes on a blank map. Visit a place they used to live. Take a ride on a vehicle similar to one that your ancestors immigrated on.

EDUCATION: Look at diplomas and academic awards of ancestors. Pretend to learn in the method they used to learn, i.e. chalkboards or quills. Memorize spelling words or poems your ancestors may have had to learn at school.

MUSIC: Learn a song that an ancestor loved. Try playing an instrument they played. Attend a concert of the same musical genre that your ancestor enjoyed.

CULTURE: Learn a dance from an ancestor's culture, cook a unique food, or wear traditional clothing. Research the holidays your ancestors celebrated and plan your own celebration.

LANGUAGE: Find a letter or journal entry of an ancestor and see if you can read their old handwriting and language. Learn some of the alphabet of your ancestor's language. Learn useful phrases in that language. Watch a show in the language of your ancestor.

TOUGH TIMES: Make pretend medals or certificates for ancestors who overcame hard things. Dress up like an ancestor, pretend to travel through a time machine, and tell your story about tough times to an audience.

WAR: Learn your ancestors' war stories. Frame their pictures, medals, or trinkets from the war. Make maps of where they served. Reenact cooking and eating with war rations. Make your own dog tags for each veteran.

MISTAKES: Make a chart with two sides. Label the first side "Choice" and the other "Consequence." Fill in the "Choice" side with your ancestor's choices and your own choices. Write decisions on pieces of a tower block game. As you remove the pieces, discuss how decisions affect our lives for better or worse and record them on the "Consequence" side.

DISCIPLINE: Try a difficult chore that an ancestor did. How has their chore or work changed in the modern day? Try doing that job yourself or visiting a place where that work is being done. Create a series of posters about jobs your ancestors had and present your findings.

RELIGION: Visit a place of worship of an ancestor's religion. Read religious texts and explore religious paintings and artifacts of ancestors' religions. Learn and present their conversion stories.

OTHER ACTIVITY IDEAS: Plan a birthday party for an ancestor. Make connecting paper dolls representing multiple generations. Plan a puppet show of an event in an ancestor's life. Learn a motto an ancestor had and make a poster. Visit a cemetery, make grave rubbings, and have a headstone scavenger hunt.

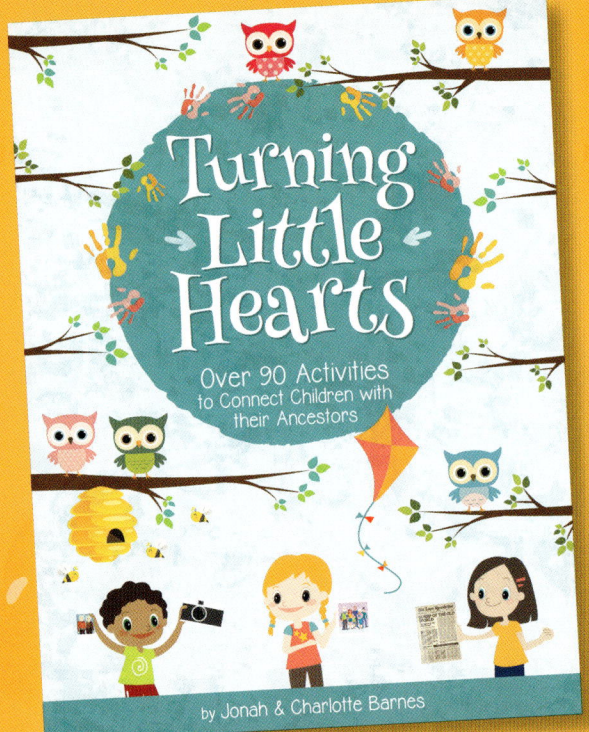

Teach your little ones

about their own ancestors with *Turning Little Hearts*, a fun and inspiring activity book also by Charlotte and Jonah Barnes.

With over 90 fun activities and storytelling templates, your children will experience their own family history in a new and exciting way.

Available at cedarfort.com, turninglittlehearts.com, Deseret Book, and Amazon.

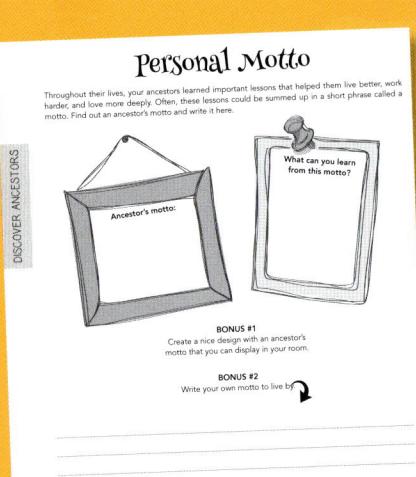
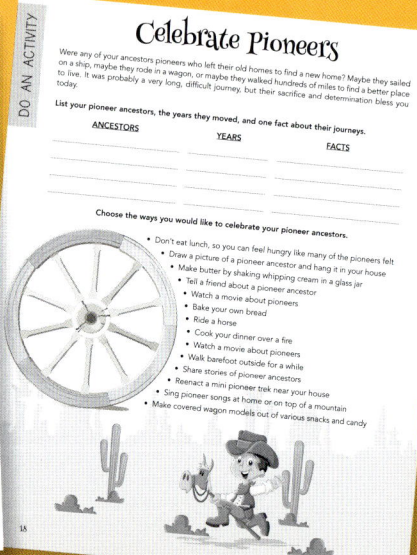
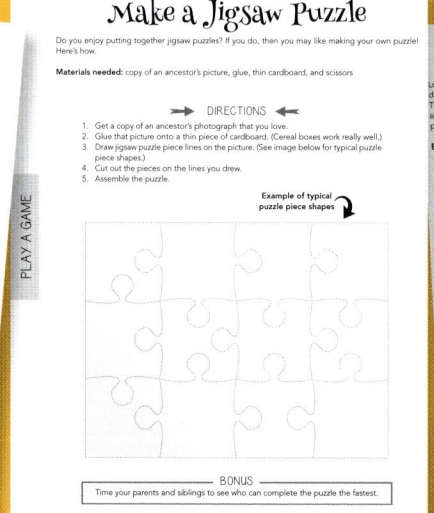
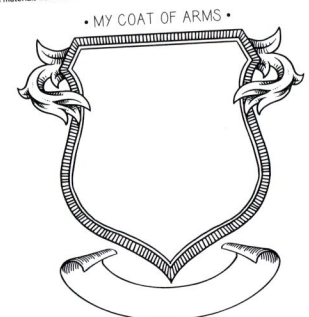